This Recipe Book belongs to:

This book or any portion thereof may not be reproduced or copied for commercial purposes without the express written permission of the author

Created by *Me Books*

Copyright © 2021 Me Books. All rights reserved.

ISBN: 9798507454020

My Recipe List

Recipe	Name
1	
2	
3	
4	
5	
6	
7	
8	
9	
10	
11	
12	
13	
14	
15	
16	
17	
18	
19	
20	
21	
22	
23	
24	
25	

Recipe	Name
26	
27	
28	
29	
30	
31	
32	
33	
34	
35	
36	
37	
38	
39	
40	
41	
42	
43	
44	
45	
46	
47	
48	
49	
50	

Recipe	Name
51	
52	
53	
54	
55	
56	
57	
58	
59	
60	
61	
62	
63	
64	
65	
66	
67	
68	
69	
70	
71	
72	
73	
74	
75	

Measurement Conversions:

Weight conversions for dry ingredients	
Imperial	Metric
1/4 oz	7g
1/2 oz	15g
1 oz	30g
2 oz	60g
3 oz	85g
4 oz	110g
5 oz	140g
6 oz	170g
7 oz	200g
8 oz	225g
9 oz	255g
10 oz	280g
11 oz	310g
12 oz	340g
13 oz	370g
14 oz	400g
15 oz	425g
1 lb	450g

Volume conversions for liquids		
Imperial	**US cups**	**Metric**
1/2 fl oz	1 tablespoon	15ml
1 fl oz	1/8 cup	30ml
2 fl oz	1/4 cup	60ml
2 1/2 fl oz	1/3 cup	80ml
4 fl oz	1/2 cup	120ml
5 fl oz	2/3 cup	160ml
6 fl oz	3/4 cup	180ml
8 fl oz	1 cup	240ml

NOTE: There's a small difference between metric cups and US cups. The standard metric cup holds 250ml of liquid whereas the US cup holds slightly less at 240ml.

Oven Conversion Chart				
Celsius °C	**Fan °C**	**Gas Mark**	**Fahrenheit °F**	**Description**
110	90	¼	225	Very slow/cool
120/130	100	½	250	Very slow/cool
140	120	1	275	Slow/cool
150	130	2	300	Slow/cool
160/170	140	3	325	Moderate/warm
180	160	4	350	Moderate
190	170	5	375	Moderately Hot
200/210	180	6	400	Fairly Hot
220	200	7	425	Hot
230	210	8	450	Very Hot
240	220	9	475	Very hot

NOTE: With fan-assisted ovens, remember to reduce the temperature by 20 degrees as shown.

Recipe 1:

Serves/Portion Size: Cooking Time:

You will need: Method:

Notes

Recipe 2:

Serves/Portion Size: .... Cooking Time:

You will need: Method:

Notes

Recipe 3:

Serves/Portion Size: Cooking Time:

You will need: Method:

Notes

Recipe 4:

Serves/Portion Size: .... Cooking Time: ....

You will need: Method:

Notes

Recipe 5:

Serves/Portion Size: .... Cooking Time: ....

You will need: Method:

Notes

Recipe 6:

Serves/Portion Size: .... Cooking Time: ....

You will need: Method:

Notes

Recipe 7:

Serves/Portion Size: Cooking Time:

You will need: Method:

Notes

Recipe 8:

Serves/Portion Size: Cooking Time:

You will need: Method:

Notes

Recipe 9:

Serves/Portion Size: Cooking Time:

You will need: Method:

Notes

Recipe 10:

Serves/Portion Size: Cooking Time:

You will need: Method:

Notes

Recipe 11:

Serves/Portion Size: Cooking Time:

You will need: Method:

Notes

Recipe 12:

Serves/Portion Size: .... Cooking Time: ....

You will need: Method:

Notes

Recipe 13:

Serves/Portion Size: Cooking Time:

You will need: Method:

Notes

Recipe 14:

Serves/Portion Size: .... Cooking Time: ....

You will need: Method:

Notes

Recipe 15:

Serves/Portion Size: .... Cooking Time: ....

You will need: Method:

Notes

Recipe 16:

Serves/Portion Size: Cooking Time:

You will need: Method:

Notes

Recipe 17:

Serves/Portion Size: .... Cooking Time: ....

You will need: Method:

Notes

Recipe 18:

Serves/Portion Size: .... Cooking Time: ....

You will need: Method:

Notes

Recipe 19:

Serves/Portion Size: .... Cooking Time: ....

You will need: Method:

Notes

Recipe 20:

Serves/Portion Size: Cooking Time:

You will need: Method:

Notes

Recipe 21:

Serves/Portion Size: Cooking Time:

You will need: Method:

Notes

Recipe 22:

Serves/Portion Size: Cooking Time:

You will need: Method:

Notes

Recipe 23:

Serves/Portion Size: .... Cooking Time: ....

You will need: Method:

Notes

Recipe 24:

Serves/Portion Size: Cooking Time:

You will need: Method:

Notes

Recipe 25:

Serves/Portion Size: .... Cooking Time: ....

You will need: Method:

Notes

Recipe 26:

Serves/Portion Size: Cooking Time:

You will need: Method:

Notes

Recipe 27:

Serves/Portion Size: Cooking Time:

You will need: Method:

Notes

Recipe 28:

Serves/Portion Size: Cooking Time:

You will need: Method:

Notes

Recipe 29:

Serves/Portion Size: .... Cooking Time: ....

You will need: Method:

Notes

Recipe 30:

Serves/Portion Size: Cooking Time:

You will need: Method:

Notes

Recipe 31:

Serves/Portion Size: _____   Cooking Time: _____

You will need: Method:

Notes

Recipe 32:

Serves/Portion Size: .... Cooking Time: ....

You will need: Method:

Notes

Recipe 33:

Serves/Portion Size: Cooking Time:

You will need: Method:

Notes

Recipe 34:

Serves/Portion Size: .... Cooking Time: ....

You will need: Method:

Notes

Recipe 35:

Serves/Portion Size: Cooking Time:

You will need: Method:

Notes

Recipe 36:

Serves/Portion Size: Cooking Time:

You will need: Method:

Notes

Recipe 37:

Serves/Portion Size: Cooking Time:

You will need: Method:

Notes

Recipe 38:

Serves/Portion Size: _____ Cooking Time: _____

You will need: Method:

Notes

Recipe 39:

Serves/Portion Size: Cooking Time:

You will need: Method:

Notes

Recipe 40:

Serves/Portion Size: Cooking Time:

You will need: Method:

Notes

Recipe 41:

Serves/Portion Size: .... Cooking Time: ....

You will need:

Method:

Notes

Recipe 42:

Serves/Portion Size: .... Cooking Time: ....

You will need: Method:

Notes

Recipe 43:

Serves/Portion Size: Cooking Time:

You will need: Method:

Notes

Recipe 44:

Serves/Portion Size: Cooking Time:

You will need: Method:

Notes

Recipe 45:

Serves/Portion Size:　　　　　　　Cooking Time:

You will need:　　　　　　　　　　Method:

Notes

Recipe 46:

Serves/Portion Size: Cooking Time:

You will need: Method:

Notes

Recipe 47:

Serves/Portion Size: Cooking Time:

You will need: Method:

Notes

Recipe 48:

Serves/Portion Size: .... Cooking Time: ....

You will need: Method:

Notes

Recipe 49:

Serves/Portion Size: Cooking Time:

You will need: Method:

Notes

Recipe 50:

Serves/Portion Size:　　　　　　　Cooking Time:

You will need:　　　　　　　　　　　Method:

Notes

Recipe 51:

Serves/Portion Size: Cooking Time:

You will need: Method:

Notes

Recipe 52:

Serves/Portion Size: Cooking Time:

You will need: Method:

Notes

Recipe 53:

Serves/Portion Size: Cooking Time:

You will need: Method:

Notes

Recipe 54:

Serves/Portion Size: .... Cooking Time: ....

You will need: Method:

Notes

Recipe 55:

Serves/Portion Size: Cooking Time:

You will need: Method:

Notes

Recipe 56:

Serves/Portion Size: Cooking Time:

You will need: Method:

Notes

Recipe 57:

Serves/Portion Size: Cooking Time:

You will need: Method:

Notes

Recipe 58:

Serves/Portion Size: Cooking Time:

You will need: Method:

Notes

Recipe 59:

Serves/Portion Size: Cooking Time:

You will need: Method:

Notes

Recipe 60:

Serves/Portion Size: Cooking Time:

You will need: Method:

Notes

Recipe 61:

Serves/Portion Size: _____   Cooking Time: _____

You will need: Method:

Notes

Recipe 62:

Serves/Portion Size: Cooking Time:

You will need: Method:

Notes

Recipe 63:

Serves/Portion Size: Cooking Time:

You will need: Method:

Notes

Recipe 64:

Serves/Portion Size: .... Cooking Time: ....

You will need: Method:

Notes

Recipe 65:

Serves/Portion Size: Cooking Time:

You will need: Method:

Notes

Recipe 66:

Serves/Portion Size: Cooking Time:

You will need: Method:

Notes

Recipe 67:

Serves/Portion Size: Cooking Time:

You will need: Method:

Notes

Recipe 68:

Serves/Portion Size: Cooking Time:

You will need: Method:

Notes

Recipe 69:

Serves/Portion Size: Cooking Time:

You will need: Method:

Notes

Recipe 70:

Serves/Portion Size: Cooking Time:

You will need: Method:

Notes

Recipe 71:

Serves/Portion Size: Cooking Time:

You will need: Method:

Notes

Recipe 72:

Serves/Portion Size: Cooking Time:

You will need: Method:

Notes

Recipe 73:

Serves/Portion Size: ....   Cooking Time: ....

You will need: Method:

Notes

Recipe 74:

Serves/Portion Size: Cooking Time:

You will need:

Method:

Notes

Recipe 75:

Serves/Portion Size: Cooking Time:

You will need: Method:

Notes

Printed in Poland
by Amazon Fulfillment
Poland Sp. z o.o., Wrocław
05 October 2021

ffed839e-a496-4f22-9000-977dc7a8d6f1R01